$old!

200+ Tips

to

Sell Your Home

for

More Money Fast

Jessica deValentino

Fascinare LLC

Fascinare books are available at a special discount when purchased in bulk. For information please write: Sales Department, Fascinare LLC, P. O. Box 420613, Houston, TX 77242 or sales@fascinare.org

Cover designs and interior design by Jessica deValentino

Library of Congress Cataloging-in-Publication Data
deValentino, Jessica

ISBN: 978-0-9828946-4-4

1. House & Home 2. Reference

2014914502

Printed and bound in the U.S.A.
10 9 8 7 6 5 4 3 2 1

Table of Contents

Disclosure

The information provided in this book is intended for informational purposes only and is not intended to constitute financial, accounting, legal, or tax advice. Many unknown factors may affect the applicability of any statement or comment within this book to your particular circumstances. You should consult directly with a local real estate agent, legal advisor, financial provider, or a tax consultant.

Over the years I have received requests for help, support, and guidance regarding the selling process, which prompted me to write this book. This guide is meant to be a simple read, one to two hours, to provide sellers more information about the selling process and how to increase the profits from the sale of their homes.

Most sellers want to net the most from the sale of their property as fast as possible. Preparing a property for the market can be a huge project, but there are simple steps that every property owner can take to help increase his or her home's value fast.

Every house is different, some are kept in pristine condition–looking picture perfect, regardless of the occasion. Other homes are more lived in and need additional preparation to be market ready.

This book addresses the important steps to take before the home hits the market, what to do while the home is on the market, and what to do after the home receives a purchase contract.

If you know the ins and outs of selling real estate, this information may be nothing new. But if you need tips and insights about how to improve your property and increase the profits generated from its sale, hopefully you will find this book insightful.

Happy selling,

Jessica
DeValentino Properties LLC
www.devalentino.com
j@devalentino.com

Chapter One
Selling

Selling a house can be a huge undertaking. Knowing what to expect throughout the selling process can help ease the anxiety sellers may feel when selling a home.

Sellers have multiple options when selling a property. A seller can manage the sale of his or her home, also known as a for sale by owner (FSBO; pronounced Fizzbo), a real estate agent can assist with the sale, an investor can purchase the property, or a home can be auctioned off to the highest bidder; each option has unique advantages and disadvantages.

For Sale by Owner

Some property owners decide to take on the entire process of selling their home. There are a variety of reasons why sellers may opt not to use a licensed real estate agent, including, but not limited to:

- Unable to find an agent
- Buyer already identified
- Avoiding a commission or fee
- Wanting complete control over the transaction (NAR, 2013).

Selling a home is not without its challenges. When polled about the most challenging tasks associated with selling their property, sellers identified the following activities:

- Attracting buyers
- Identifying repair efforts
- Properly pricing the property
- Completing required paperwork
- Effectively marketing the property
- Assisting buyers to obtain financing
- Effectively managing the entire transaction (NAR, 2013).

Real Estate Agent

Having a good supportive real estate agent can help make the selling process a lot easier. Real estate agents are knowledgeable of the requirements of real estate transactions and network with other real estate agents to possibly get a faster sale and more profits. Overall, hiring the right real estate agent may save time, effort, frustration, and money.

Real estate agents may take on three different roles during home sale transactions, which include: listing agent, buyer's agent, and intermediary. Each of these roles facilitates the real estate transaction in different ways.

Sellers contact listing agents to sell their home. The listing agent then lists and markets the home for sale. A home for sale is also known as a listing.

Some buyers may search on their own to find a property to buy, but this may require contacting multiple real estate agents to view each property; not fun. It seems easier to find one real estate agent to work with throughout the home buying journey, and this is what most buyers do. Buyer's agents assist buyers in purchasing property.

The third and final role is the intermediary role. An intermediary real estate agent works for both the buyer and seller in one transaction; it can be challenging to adequately serve the needs of both the seller and the buyer in the same transaction.

A good real estate agent will provide a multitude of services including, but not limited to:

- ❖ Staging assistance.
- ❖ Secure lockbox showings.
- ❖ Comparative Market Analysis (CMA).
- ❖ Reduce liability by avoiding selling pitfalls.
- ❖ Arrange property showings and inspections.
- ❖ Network with agents to facilitate the sale.
- ❖ Provide showing feedback & progress reports.
- ❖ Negotiate with buyers or other real estate agents.
- ❖ Assistance with contracts, financing, and closing.
- ❖ Sell property faster, while saving time & money. (NAR, 2013)

Each state has varying rules and regulations regarding the buying, selling, renting, and leasing of real estate. The sale of real estate often requires forms and contracts, some of which include, but are not limited to: the purchase contract, lead-based paint addendum, and third-party financing addendum. Knowledgeable real estate agents can help sellers to reduce liability, while facilitating the sale of a property.

Selling a home can be a time consuming process. A good real estate agent can help save an immense amount of time by filtering calls from buyers or nosey neighbors, showing your property, and networking with other real estate agents to increase the odds of receiving a good offer.

Pricing a property right can be challenging. Real estate agents generally perform comparative market analysis to determine a good price point. A comparative market analysis reviews the salient information regarding recently sold properties and properties currently on the market to develop a good price to market the property, also known as the listing price.

Most real estate agents have seen numerous properties; giving them a good idea of how a properly staged home looks. It may be beneficial to have a real estate agent view the home and offer suggestions to enhance the appearance of the property.

In the past, many real estate agents used combination lockboxes to secure the keys of properties listed for sale. When buyer's agents wanted to show the property to their clients, the combination was provided by the listing agent.

Now there are electronic lockboxes, which are definitely more secure than the combination lockboxes of the past. Most real estate agents have an electronic key to open lockboxes. The electronic lockbox also records each real estate agent who accesses the lockbox; providing additional security to the home. Generally the lockboxes are defaulted to only allow access to a property between certain time frames like 8:00 a.m. and 9:00 p.m., but these time frames may be adjusted.

While real estate agents do charge a commission, having a good real estate agent can more than cover the expense of their commission. In 2013, approximately 10% of owners sold their homes without the assistance of a real estate agent. Typically homes sold by owners sold for $184,000, while homes sold with the assistance of a real estate agent sold for approximately $230,000; over $45,000 more! (NAR, 2014)

Real estate agents generally earn a commission based off of the sales price of a property. Commissions are typically paid by the seller at closing, and the commission is split between the listing and buyer's agent. Real estate brokers may charge varying commission percentages; all of the details regarding the commissions should be spelled out in the listing agreement.

The buyer of your home may have a real estate agent representing his or her interests, consider obtaining your own representation as well; someone knowledgeable who will facilitate the transaction on your behalf.

Investors

If your home needs some work and you do not want to invest the time and effort necessary to make your property market ready, consider targeting an investor.

Generally, investors are willing to take on the challenge of preparing a home for the market. Everything is a trade-off, while an investor is willing to take a property in less than stellar condition, he or she may not be willing to pay full price for this opportunity. Most likely the investor will want to have a significant discount.

Investors generally look for a property that has the potential to be great with a little TLC. Investors purchase, quickly renovate and enhance the property, and put the property back on the market. The price of the investment property must allow the investor to recoup the property's purchase price, renovation costs, and generate a nice profit. The process of quickly buying, renovating, and reselling property for a profit is also popularly known as flipping a house.

When specifically targeting investors, use the right descriptions to catch their eye. Words like:

- Fixer-upper
- Lots of potential
- Needs a little TLC
- Handyman's special
- Great investment property

Using the right descriptors can help buyers looking for move-in ready homes to steer clear from investment properties, while beckoning those who are interested in doing a little work for a potentially great opportunity.

Be forewarned, most investors are looking for great deals and bottom of the barrel prices. An investor's purchase offer may be significantly less than you expected, even from an investor. After hearing offers from a couple of investors, you may just want to put in the effort to sell your home to a traditional buyer.

Auctions

An auction is a good selling strategy to use when a seller wants a quick sell and profit is less of issue. In order to be successful a wide net must be cast to capture the attention of the most bidders.

Under optimal conditions, a real estate auction can bring in great profits. Ideally, numerous bidders drive up the price of the property at an auction; culminating in the highest bidder winning the property.

While a real estate auction may be a fast way to sale a home, it precludes the participation of traditional home buyers who utilize third party lenders to finance properties. Auctions generally require 100% cash funding immediately after the bidding closes; this is not an option for most traditional buyers.

Sellers have multiple options to secure the sale of their property. It is important to consider the advantages and disadvantages associated with each option to make an informed decision about the sale of a property.

Action Steps

_____

_____

_____

_____

_____

_____

_____

_____

_____

_____

_____

_____

_____

_____

_____

_____

_____

_____

Chapter Two
Cleaning

Clean is just a starting point when selling a property–make it sparkle. Even the slightest distraction can turn off a buyer. Applying a little more effort may bring you better offers.

When was that last time that your home was cleaned from floor to ceiling? If it has been more than a couple of weeks, that is too long.

There are thousands of nooks and crannies inside of every home and each one needs to be cleaned and sanitized to present the best image to buyers.

Sometimes sellers want to test the market by placing a home on the market before it is actually ready to see how the market will respond to the property; this may not be the best idea. Many people, especially real estate agents, watch and track how often homes are listed for sale. If a property is repeatedly on the market, it may signify that a home has problems selling and there may be issues with the home. If the home is listed for sale in a multiple listing service (MLS), a database used to market properties, real estate agents can track how often a home has been on the market over the years and how long it took the property to sale; and real estate agents may use this information to their advantage.

Clean

Cleaning a home before putting it up for sale seems like an obvious step; however, too much attention cannot be paid to the cleanliness of a home. A buyer is making one of the biggest investments of his or her life; therefore, it is crucial to make the best impression possible. Anything can turn a buyer off and cause him or her not to make an offer. Clean everything from ceiling to floor and everything in between. And when you're finished cleaning everything, clean everything once more to be sure.

Remember that no room is off limits; every single space within the property lines is important. Buyers will open every single drawer, closet, room, and especially the garage. There is literally nowhere to hide your stuff in your home anymore.

Depersonalize

There are two schools of thought regarding depersonalizing a home. On one hand, you want to show that a family lives in the home and it is a great place. Knick-knacks, family heirlooms, and photos tell a story and buyers may feel a sense of family and a connection to your home.

On the other hand, buyers want to envision their family, not your family in the home. Seeing photos and remnants of your family may prevent the buyer from truly connecting to the property.

You want buyers to envision themselves in your home; help buyers envision themselves there. Pack up your special effects and family photos, and get your belongings ready for a new home.

Declutter

If you are like the average person, you have collected a lot of stuff over the years. You may have so much stuff that you forgot that you even had it. While it is great to have wonderful things, too much stuff can prevent your home from showing well.

You may need to make some tough decisions about what to keep and what to throw away. Decluttering your home can make it more presentable and attractive to buyers.

If you are not using items on a regular basis, you may want to remove the items from the home before it goes on the market. But you may not have to throw it away. Consider storing or giving some of your belongings to friends or family, this way you can visit or even retrieve your possessions after the sale of your property.

In some areas, consignment shops are making a comeback. Consignment shops will place your items for sale and pay you a portion of the profits when they sell. This could be a great way to earn a little extra cash.

If consigning is not right for you, consider giving your old things an entirely new life by donating them to others who may really need them. The Salvation Army, Goodwill, and other charitable organizations are always looking for donations and your donations may count as a tax write off; make sure to ask for a receipt and put it in a safe place until tax season.

Where Do I Put My Stuff?

With buyers looking at every single inch of your home, you may be wondering where to put your stuff. You are moving, so if possible move to your new home. This may help your home show better to buyers.

Perhaps you are not quite ready to move before you receive an offer, but you really may need to reduce the amount of stuff in your home. Then you might consider getting a storage unit. A storage unit will allow you to keep your stuff, while reducing the clutter of your home during the selling process.

If you can't possibly part with your prized possessions for an extended period of time, consider getting a moveable storage unit. The storage units resemble large sturdy steel crates typically seen on trains and large cargo ships. Some moveable storage units include Pack Rat, My Way, and Pods. The moveable storage company will even transport the storage unit to your new residence. While the unit may be a bit unsightly sitting in your driveway, your stuff will be close and out of the way.

Whatever you decide, make sure that your home is clean and clutter free. A couple of moveable storage companies include, but are not limited to:

www.1800packrat.com
www.pods.com
www.upack.com

Check your local area to find more moveable storage companies.

Deodorize

After you have cleaned, depersonalized, and decluttered, check to see if the house smells clean. It can be hard to be 100% objective about the smell of your house, after all it is your house–you may not be able to smell the scent of your home.

It is referred to by a series of names including, but not limited to: scent blindness, olfactory memory, and olfactory habituation; whereas one devotes less attention and responsiveness to a familiar smell and may not even recognize certain scents because the senses have become accustomed to certain smells.

Nonetheless, it is imperative to have a fresh smelling home. When trying to deodorize a home consider the following:

1. Paint
2. Gel scent absorbers
3. Spray can deodorizers
4. Open the windows and doors
5. Thoroughly clean the furniture
6. Wash and sanitize the walls, windows, doors, and floors

Garage

The garage, also known as the biggest closet in the house, should be impeccably cleaned; it should not be the storage area for everything from the house. The garage should be neatly organized. Clean and organized spaces often appear more spacious and accommodating, versus spaces that are packed to the gills, which may appear stuffy and small.

Pressure Wash

Over the years, dirt, mold, mildew, and grime can accumulate on your home's driveway, brick, wood, and sidewalk. Dull and dark surfaces scream old and uncared for, which can significantly distract from the beauty of your home. Before you have buyers viewing your property, consider having the exterior of the property thoroughly cleansed with a good pressure washing. Pressure washing is a great way to brighten the exterior surfaces of your home.

"Move In" Ready

After you have depersonalized, decluttered, cleansed, and deodorized every single inch of your house, it may be "move in" ready. That means that the buyer will not have to make one single alteration to move into a fantastic home. The buyer will turn the key, and voila! The buyer's new home is ready.

Thoroughly cleaning a home can be a big undertaking, but it is not only an important part of getting a home ready to show, it is important for a new family as well. For more information, review the appendix to find a deep cleaning checklist and daily cleaning checklist. Both of which can be downloaded from www.devalentino.com.

Action Steps

Chapter Three
Inside /
Outside

To net the highest profits from selling a home it is paramount to adequately prepare your property for the market. A home should be in optimal condition as soon as it hits the market.

It can be challenging to be objective about your home. After all, it is your home, you should think it is wonderful. But thinking your home is wonderful may blind you to the blatant flaws that can prevent you from getting the best offer, or any offer at all. Therefore, it is crucial to get a second, if not third, fourth, or fifth opinion about the current condition of your home.

Ask your friends, family, and a real estate agent to be completely honest about the condition of your home to identify areas for possible improvements; this is a good way to get your home in tip-top condition. This thorough inspection should not be limited to the inside of the house, but should extend outside as well.

While feedback can be uncomfortable to hear, this is no time to be sensitive; you want brutally honest feedback. Keep in mind that feedback is a subjective opinion; you may not always agree with the feedback that you receive; however, at the very least consider the feedback. Feedback can help you correct potential issues within your home before buyers view it.

Walk around the perimeter of the house; be nit-picky–inspect every inch of the exterior of the house. The exterior check should include everything from the fence, siding, garage, gutters, grass, and driveway. What is the condition of the exterior brick, HardiePlank, stucco, or wood? Are all outside materials in-tact and painted well? Are the windows and doors in-tact and sufficiently caulked?

Next, move onto the interior of the property. Going in an orderly fashion from room to room, inspect the condition of each room from floor to ceiling. Specifically, you are looking for cracks, stains, or sagging, which can be an indicator of additional issues. When you identify any issues, investigate and resolve them.

Purchasing a home is a huge investment; most buyers will purchase the most home that they can afford, leaving little money for updates and repairs. Buyers want to know that they are making a sound investment, not buying a problematic money pit that requires countless repairs.

A house needing numerous repairs may scare off some buyers. In addition, in the purchase contract some buyers will require the seller to make repairs before closing. Some lenders also may require the seller to make repairs before closing. Completing numerous repairs before closing can be stressful to the seller. It is better if all repairs are made before the home actually hits the market.

Some real estate agents and buyers reduce the purchase offer incrementally for every single issue identified in the property; justifying the reduction by the condition of the property. To help avoid a reduced offer, make every effort to fix all issues within the property.

You should make every attempt to repair every item within the home before it goes on the market. Making the needed repairs can help to bring in the best possible offer and can help buyers to feel more comfortable, like they have found a really well-taken care of home.

After you have completed your inspections, completed the repairs, and spruced up your home as much as possible– consider taking the inspection process a bit further by hiring a property inspector.

You might be thinking, isn't the inspection the responsibility of the buyer? Yes, most buyers will order their own property inspection. Unfortunately a property inspector's report can damage, even ruin a deal.

In addition, waiting until the buyers conduct a property inspection and demand small repairs can slow the closing process. Get a property inspection as soon as possible and make the repairs to ensure that your property is in tip-top condition.

A property inspector can provide you with a more detailed picture about the state of your property. Depending on the maintenance that you have performed on the property, the repair list may not be extensive.

Generally, property inspectors demonstrate their value by identifying every single thing that is wrong with the property, which can be overwhelming for some buyers; causing them to abandon the purchase contract. Some of the property issues identified by the property inspector may be very small items, and even nit-picky. Don't let small issues ruin your contract, fix them before the home is placed on the market.

After completing the suggestions and repairs identified by the property inspector, consider getting a final inspection to share with buyers to demonstrate the property's clean bill of health.

First Impression

Your home may not get a second chance to make a first impression. Take full advantage of every opportunity that your home is given. Wow the buyers who visit your home. As soon as buyers arrive at your home make them say, "Wow!"

Like it or not, your house will be judged on appearance, cleanliness, and more. When buyers drive up to your home you want them to think, "Looks good! I can't wait to see the inside!" Curb appeal is important and can help homes to sale faster than value and price (NAR, 2013).

Neighborhood

Your home's neighborhood is almost as important as the home itself, and to some people the neighborhood may be even more important.

When you decide to move, look around at the homes in your neighborhood; buyers may do so as well. If your neighbors' homes are not in prime condition, consider asking them if they would like your help. Helping your neighbors can be as simple as cutting their yard, collecting their newspapers, or trimming their hedges. When you help your neighbors, you may help yourself as well.

Curb and Address Markers

Make it easy for buyers to immediately find your property by ensuring that your home's curb and address markers are easily visible from the street. Over the years the curb and street markers can become faded. Retouching or replacing the markers can help buyers to easily find your home.

If you determine that your curb and address markers are in need of repair, your neighborhood hardware store will likely have the materials to help you make the updates.

Yard

After ensuring that the home can be easily identified with clear curb and address markers, ensure that the front yard is impeccably manicured. The front yard is one of the first sights that buyers see when they arrive to your home.

Landscaping can be a small cost, yet it is one of the most important tasks to help sell a house. An analysis of real estate sales reported that beautifying the landscaping of a property can help it to sell 20% faster (NAR, 2013). Beautifying a front yard can be as easy a quick trip to the plant and garden center and a few hours of gardening.

It is paramount to keep the property nicely manicured while on the market, which does not take much; healthy trimmed green grass, neatly trimmed trees and bushes, and a couple of potted plants if you are feeling adventurous.

If you are not living in the property, it may be necessary to hire a lawn service to regularly maintain the yard; this is definitely worth the added expense.

Mailbox

Like the yard, the mailbox is one of the first things that a buyer may notice as he or she approaches your home. Make sure the mailbox makes a good impression. Whether it is a new coat of paint or a brand new mailbox, ensure the mailbox adds to the value of the home.

Pest Control

Taking the necessary precautions to eliminate any unsightly pests and vermin is crucial. Spraying pesticides around the perimeter of the home to eliminate bugs and ants is a good precautionary measure to ensure there are not any unwelcomed visitors inside of the property.

Fences

Over time, fences can become old, dingy, and even loose.
Carefully check the boards of the fence to ensure they are
secure. In addition, if needed, consider power washing the fence
to bring back its original look.

Conducting a thorough inspection of the interior and
exterior of the property can help to identify potential issues with
the property and give you the opportunity to resolve any
identified issues before buyers visit and view it.

Action Steps

_____

_____

_____

_____

_____

_____

_____

_____

_____

_____

_____

_____

_____

_____

_____

_____

_____

_____

_____

Chapter Four
Beyond Repairs

You have depersonalized, decluttered, cleaned, personally and professionally inspected your home, but you still are not satisfied with its condition. You are contemplating whether or not to make additional alterations to your home in hopes of bringing in higher purchase offers. This is a very big decision that should receive adequate deliberation.

On the other hand, sellers may not want to invest a lot of money into their current property because they are focusing on saving money to move to their new property; after all, sellers need a new place to live. But in order to reap the most profits it is imperative to make the home look as good as possible.

Shortcomings

Some sellers are already aware that their homes may have one or more shortcomings. Some common shortcomings include: old paint, old carpet, and outdated styles. Instead of the correcting the shortcomings, some sellers offer buyers an allowance.

For instance, Betty the seller, knows that the carpet inside of her home is horrific, but she decides not to replace it.

Betty is strapped for money, and believes she has already invested enough money into the property and she does not want to invest a single penny more.

Betty decides to offer a $2,000 carpet allowance in lieu of replacing the carpet. Betty thinks this is a great idea. Offering a carpet allowance allows Betty to keep her money until closing, at which point the $2,000 will come out of the proceeds from the sale of the home. Besides, Betty believes that waiting will allow the buyers to pick their own color or perhaps even wood floors. *Who doesn't love hardwoods floors?*

Theoretically, Betty has a point; the buyers may not like her carpet selection. The problem lies in the fact that most buyers can't see pass the existing ugly carpet. Ugly carpet may stop the buyers from falling in love with the property and making an offer. Yes, there is the abstract $2,000 allowance to purchase the carpet, but it is not visible.

In addition, Betty and the buyer both know that replacing the carpet may cost a lot more than $2,000. So the allowance may fail to satisfy the buyers.

Don't expect the buyer to make improvements to your property. Moving is already a huge undertaking. An allowance requires the buyer to do even more work to make the property move-in ready.

There is a buyer who is willing to accept your home with all of its flaws, an investor. For accepting your home in less than perfect condition, an investor expects to receive a deep discount, which may cost more than the needed improvements.

In order to reap the highest profits from the sale of your home, make sure that it is worth the expense. Don't expect the buyer to give you a full price offer and do all of the work to make your property great; it generally doesn't go both ways. Buyers are more willing to part with their hard-earned cash when they see a great property. If you want top-dollar, provide a quality product.

Visit Properties

See an open house sign in your neighborhood, take the opportunity to go in and look around to check out your competition. Check out the price and amenities provided within the property. Looking at a few homes in your neighborhood can give you a better idea of your competition and the standard amenities within the homes. Monitor how long the properties in your neighborhood are on the market. Keep this information in mind while preparing your property for the market.

Updates, Upgrades, Renovations, & Remodels

It is paramount to take the needed steps to beautify one's home and make it more attractive to buyers. Adequately preparing the home for sale may reduce the amount of time the home spends on the market.

Unkempt homes can languish for extended periods of time on the market. Buyer's agents may look at the property's days on market (DOM). If a house has spent an extended period of time on the market, it may signify that no one else is interested in the property and the buyer may offer less than the full asking price for the property.

Small alterations can greatly enhance the appearance of a property. There are varying degrees of home improvements, which include updating, upgrading, renovating, and remodeling. Updating, upgrading, renovating, and remodeling each have the potential to enhance the value of your property and bring additional profits from its sale.

Alterations to a property can be costly. In addition, a seller may not be able to recoup all of the funds invested into the property. Consider all of the advantages and disadvantages associated with each option to make the choice that is right for you and your property. When funds are limited, it is crucial to determine where they would be best spent.

Carefully choose projects that will result in the most value. The National Association of Realtors reports that siding, kitchens remodeling, and window replacements are worthy renovations; allowing homeowners to recoup 80% or more of their investment during a resale (2013).

Alterations can definitely separate your home from the competition and help it to stand out to the buyers. But it is important to consider how the alterations compare to other properties in the neighborhood. Consider if buyers may be willing to pay for the alterations. Consider if you may be able to recoup your investment.

Reviewing recent sales in a neighborhood may provide a good indicator of how much buyers may be willing to pay for a property and special amenities within the property. What do other homes in your area have? What do the base, average, and high-end models sale for?

For instance, if you find a home that has 40k in renovations, but it only sold for 10k more than a base model home, then significant alterations may not be a good investment.

Older properties may benefit from updating or replacing outdated fixtures and appliances. For instance, the appearance of a home may be greatly enhanced by replacing dated wood paneling, shag carpet, and colored sinks and tubs popular in the past.

Upgrades can really enhance the appearance of a room. For instance, there is a perfectly good laminate countertop. The countertop does not need repair and is not outdated, but an upgrade to granite would enhance the overall appearance of the countertops and the kitchen.

A renovation generally involves the renewal of some aspect of the home, perhaps painting the wall or refinishing the floors or cabinets. The most major alterations generally occur during a remodel. A remodel may alter the structure and or style of an area of the property or the entire property. For example, a remodel may involve knocking out a wall to open up and expand the kitchen.

Paint

At a minimum, it is important to go through the home and patch and paint the walls to ensure they are knick and dent free. In addition, a fresh coat of paint can do wonders for a home's appearance. Paint can cover all of the bumps and bruises that a home endures throughout the years.

Don't provide a paint allowance, don't wait until you get an offer, and don't sloppily slap some paint up. Have a fresh coat of paint applied to showcase your home.

If you have outdated wallpaper, consider removing it and select a neutral paint palette that will blend easily with any furniture.

Sometimes there is contradictory information about wall color. Some realtors and interior design experts profess that wall colors are evil and may not appeal to buyers. While others insist that wall color enhances, even enlivens a room.

As we all know everyone has unique and personal taste. While a color may be beautiful to one person, it may be distasteful to another. For instance, Suzy loved the light mossy green colored walls, but Luke said the color looked like snot.

While a room's color is not permanent, it is something that a buyer will have to live with day in and out until the room is repainted. When selecting colors, remember that buyers can have strong aversions to certain colors.

Buyers generally do not have strong aversions to neutral colors. A neutral wall palette is generally recommended because it has the ability to appeal to the most buyers. Whereas, vibrant and distinct color palettes may only appeal to a few buyers. Creams, taupes, and beiges offer a tinge of color without being too overwhelming to most buyers.

Fixtures

Light fixtures can be an easy way to spruce up a room. If your light fixtures are outdated, consider replacing them. Your local hardware or home improvement store may have a variety of beautiful and economical options to help update your fixtures. Quick note: gold or brass fixtures were popular in the past. Consider silver, nickel, bronze, chrome, or stainless steel for a more updated look.

Cabinetry

New kitchen and bathroom cabinets can definitely add a dazzling touch to a room; but removing the old cabinets, purchasing the new cabinets, and installing new cabinets can be quite costly. Not to mention purchasing new countertops. There are several options that can help uplift a kitchen or bathroom, without putting as big of a dent in your wallet.

The first option is staining or painting the cabinetry. Staining or painting the cabinets is a nice way to enhance them. In combination with new hardware, like knobs or pulls, your kitchen or bathroom can be stunning.

Instead of replacing the entire cabinet, if the body of the cabinet is good, consider only replacing the cabinet doors. Replacing the cabinet doors offers a great face lift to the cabinets, at a fraction of the cost of replacing the entire cabinet.

Replacing the cabinet doors is an especially good option, if you have already installed granite or equally expensive countertops. Replacing the laminate countertops with granite countertops is another good way to enhance the cabinets, countertops, and the room.

Flooring

Worn out carpeting and distressed flooring can be a huge turn-off to buyers; however, fantastic looking floors can really catch a buyer's attention. Many people prefer the beauty and cleanliness of hardwood floors.

Carpet can hold smells, stains, and pet hair. At the very least, carpet should be shampooed or steamed cleaned before a property is placed on the market. Replacing the carpet with new flooring is even better.

Outbuilding

Outbuilding occurs when the updates, upgrades, renovations, and or renovations completed in the property significantly surpass other properties in the neighborhood. Think of building a French style palace with marble floors, diamond chandeliers, and a million dollars of plush landscaping in a neighborhood with the average home value of $35k and the highest home value of $40k. Any seller would likely have a hard time recouping the millions of dollars invested developing the property.

While the example of a French style palace in low property value neighborhood is a dramatic over-the-top example, this occurrence happens on a smaller scale every day across the country. Homeowners, invest large amounts of money into their homes and when it is time to sell, they want to recoup their investment.

The problem occurs when the seller's neighbors have not made the same investment in their property. So while outbuilders may get top dollar for their home, there may be a limit to that top dollar amount and trying to recapture all of the money invested in the home may cause it to sit on the market for an extended period of time. And in some regretful situations, the home may never receive an offer during the listing period.

When buyers purchase a property they are not only purchasing the property, but they are also purchasing a stake in the neighborhood and the surrounding area. Most buyers want a home in an equally nice neighborhood. Buyers will most likely not want to buy a mansion in a village of shacks.

Granted, buyers may recognize the extra enhancements of the home, and some may be willing to pay for them; but it is important to have realistic expectations regarding your neighborhood and home. The alterations that you have made must be valuable to buyers in order for them to be willing to pay for them.

Keep in mind that not all alterations to a property will increase its value. Some alterations are just a personal preference. While the alteration may be valuable to the seller, it may not have as much or any value to a buyer. Sellers tend to overestimate the value of alterations to their property, which can be counterproductive to the sale of the property.

Alterations can really enhance the appearance of a property. It is important to carefully consider the neighborhood, your funds, and your property to make the best decision regarding updating, upgrading, renovating, or remodeling.

Action Steps

Chapter Five
Staging

After everything is cleaned, decluttered, and depersonalized and, fixed up–it is time to dazzle! Let's face it, not everyone is creative or has vision; this may include the buyers. Luckily, there is staging. Staging reveals a property's potential to buyers. An analysis of real estate sales reports that professionally staged homes can sell 20-40% faster (NAR, 2013).

New home builders frequently stage their homes; filling them with furniture and styling everything exquisitely to help the home achieve the perfect look.

Whether you have great furniture or not, you can easily stage your home. When staging, remember that less is more. You want to give a buyer a sense of how the room is going to feel, without overstuffing it.

Most people generally have too much furniture in their homes; they have their original furniture, a couple of new pieces, and a couple of heirlooms collected on the journey of life. After a while, a home can be filled to the brim with furniture, which may prevent the home from truly shining.

Too much furniture can make a home look small and cramped. A buyer may think, if your home cannot accommodate all of your stuff; how on earth will it accommodate all of mine?

Entryway

Make it your mission to comb through your house neatly organizing anything and everything. When in doubt, throw it out; this will most likely facilitate your moving process while making your home look larger and visually appealing.

The entryway should be warm and welcoming. After being thoroughly cleansed, consider applying a fresh coat of enamel paint to the door. New door hardware can be purchased relatively inexpensively and can really improve the appearance of the front door.

In addition, with buyers on the brink of arriving at your home, consider placing a new welcome mat at the front door. Potted flowers can also be a welcoming sight.

Kitchen

For most people, the kitchen is one of the most important rooms of the home. Spending a little extra time organizing and styling the kitchen can transforms it into a spectacular spot.

Buyers are likely to open the cabinets, pantry, refrigerator, oven, and dishwasher. It is important to ensure that behind every door and pull of the drawer is a well-organized space. Line up the boxes and the containers neatly; think Laura from the movie *Sleeping with the Enemy.*

Carefully consider the size of the table and chairs; oversized tables and chairs can make a room look smaller. If needed, reduce the size of the table by removing the leaf. If there are too many chairs, move some of them to storage; this can help the kitchen to look larger and more spacious.

The sink can quickly become overrun with sponges, cloths, rags, soap, and other cleaners. Consider removing all of the cleaners and utensils to help the sink look neat and organized. Always clean and put away dishes; a sink with dirty dishes attracts flies and leaves unpleasant smells.

The typical kitchen can be overrun with gadgets, utensils, and appliances like the toaster, coffee maker, juicer, etc. Consider which appliances are absolutely necessary. Remove all infrequently used appliances, while frequently used appliances should be stored in a cabinet or pantry; this will help the kitchen appear more spacious.

Make sure that the refrigerator is cleansed on the inside and the outside. The exterior of the refrigerator often can be overrun with too many items like magnets, photos, or notes. On the inside, consider removing any old, expired, or infrequently used food and wash down the surfaces to make them sparkle.

Once you have decluttered the kitchen, it should look more spacious, but perhaps a little bare. Consider using cookbooks, fruits, plants, or decorative items to fill and enhance the appearance of the kitchen.

Dining Room

Most buyers want a dining room, so make one. Whether it is a formal dining room or an impromptu space that houses a dining table. A dining room should be comfortable and inviting; encouraging buyers to see themselves and their loved ones gathered to dine.

It is not necessary to go overboard and over accessorize to create an appealing dining area. Consider adding a few pieces such as place settings of two or more, a vase with fresh flowers, a mirror, and artwork; these items can be great additions to help stage a dining room.

Bedroom

When decorating the bedroom, remember that less is more. The bedroom can be easily transformed into a tranquil sanctuary by decluttering and removing as much of the stuff in the bedroom as possible.

Instantly enhance the bedroom by refreshing the paint with a nice neutral color, and selecting a great color scheme for the bedding, pillows, and the window treatments.

If your bedroom furniture is a bit dated or worn, consider removing it from the bedroom. A bedroom really doesn't need that much furniture to be complete; a bed with a headboard and a night stand or two. A nice headboard can add elegance and sophistication to a bedroom. There may be an additional piece of furniture or two, but remember, the more furniture that you have in the bedroom, the smaller that the bedroom may appear. Carefully evaluate the furniture that you really need. When in doubt, take it out.

To build on your staging, consider adding a breakfast tray on the bed with an empty coffee cup, saucer, napkin, and newspaper. This may conjure pleasant thoughts in the minds of the buyers.

Children's Room

Keeping a child's room in optimal showing condition can definitely be a challenge; however, with your help, a wonderful room can be easier for a child to maintain. Consider removing or reducing the quantity of toys and furniture from the room. In addition, implementing a cleaning game to encourage your child to keep the room clean may be fun.

Living Room

The living room should look cozy and inviting. To style the living room, keep the sofas off the walls; this may help to make the room look larger.

Consider removing all non-essential furniture to maximize the space. Neatly arrange anything that may be left out like remotes, games systems, magazines, pillows, and throws.

Bathrooms

A bathroom can be easily transformed into a tranquil retreat with the addition of new shower curtains, trash receptacles, and an ornate mirror.

Take a page out the hotel make-ready handbook by hanging a plush robe on a hook and placing a grouping of soaps, lotions, and shampoos on the countertop; this can help the bathroom to look more picturesque.

Closets

Almost everyone wants and needs more closet space. However, filling up closets can make them look small and cramped. When cleaning the house and reducing the clutter, it can be very tempting to place everything in the closet, but don't. Showcase the closets with all of their grandeur by keeping them as empty as possible. This will allow buyers to see the spaciousness of the closets and allow them to envision how their possessions will fit into the space.

Plants

In addition to beautifying a home, plants have additional positive qualities, including, but not limited to:

- Increasing humidity
- Reducing airborne dust levels
- Keeping air temperatures down
- Reducing carbon dioxide levels
- Reducing levels of certain pollutants (Ambius, 2014).

Take advantage of all of the benefits that plants offer. Consider placing potted plants and vases of flowers throughout the house to create an amazing atmosphere.

Light

Every inch of your home should be light and bright; banish the darkness. Start by checking and replacing ever single light bulb in your home. Next, open the windows to let the natural light in. In addition, hanging a mirror across from a window will reflect natural light and brighten a room.

Windows can be dressed up relatively inexpensively with the addition of blinds, curtain rods, and or curtain panels. When selecting window treatments remember that neutral colors have the ability to appeal to more buyers.

Flow

It is important that a home has adequate space for movement. Walk through the house to ensure that the furniture does not impede the buyers as they move throughout the house.

Showcase the spaciousness of a room. Consider rearranging the furniture to facilitate movement in tight areas. Buyers need to be able to move around the house and not feel blocked into a space. All walkways should have adequate room for people to easily move throughout the house.

Odd Room

Sometimes homes may have an odd room. A room may not be a bedroom, nor have a specific purpose; this can confuse buyers. Don't confuse the buyers, you can easily clarify the purpose of a room by turning it into an office. Almost everyone can easily identify with the need to have a home office; a place to organize files and folders and store books. And don't forget the pièce de résistance, the desk. A desk signifies to most people–this is an office.

Staging a home is an important part of the selling process. Staging helps sellers to systematically review and set each areas of the home; thereby maximizing the home's ability to show well to buyers.

Action Steps

_____

_____

_____

_____

_____

_____

_____

_____

_____

_____

_____

_____

_____

_____

_____

_____

_____

_____

_____

_____

_____

Chapter Six
Incentive$

In a highly competitive buyers' market, incentives can help give real estate agents and buyers the added motivation to select your property. There are a number of strategies that buyers can employ to improve the odds of getting an offer.

A seller may need to sale a home at supersonic lightning speed, but generally this should be top-secret information. A "must sell" home and "motivated seller" can signify distress. Distress signifies problems, which can be unattractive and a repellant to buyers. Words like "must sell" and "motivated seller" may attract investors, but investors generally do not offer the most attractive or lucrative deals. Carefully phrase the description of the property; every word counts.

BTSA

Creating an incentive to sell your property is a good way to motivate real estate agents to show your property. When real estate agents look in the database of available properties, they try to select the properties that may interest their clients. Every so often, a real estate agent may run across a property that advertises BTSA - Bonus to Selling Agent. This means at closing, there is a bonus for the agent who sales the property. This gives the buyer's agent an extra incentive to show, promote, and sell a property.

Seller Financing

Offering financing is a great way to facilitate the sale of your home, while offering extra benefits to you as the seller and the buyer.

Benefits to the seller may include, but are not limited to: a faster closing, ability to net more overtime, and a larger pool of buyers. Benefits to the buyer may include, but are not limited to: an opportunity for the buyer to rebuild his or her credit, the opportunity to purchase a home, and the avoidance of costly fees associated with third party financing.

When a buyer obtains third party financing, the lender provides the entire sum to the seller, minus any money owed to lienholders, to create a free and clear title. But this large lump sum of money may be heavily taxed; thereby, effectively reducing the lump sum.

In some cases, the seller may net more over life of the loan when the buyer repays the principal and interest. The before mentioned lump sum payment is only principal. In a traditional sale of a $200,000 property, the seller receive a check from the buyer or lender, minus any liens owed to cover the price of the property. Done deal; 200k even.

But when the seller is the financier at 7%, the seller will get 200k and 279k in interest over 30 years.

Mortgage Repayment Summary

$1,330.60	$479,017.80
Monthly Payment	Total of 360 Payments

Total Interest Paid Over 30 Years: $279,017.80

When the seller provides the financing, the seller may be able to set a higher purchase price and higher interest rate, which can generate more profits in comparison to the cash offer or third party pay-off.

Seller financing may be particularly attractive to buyers who have no credit, self-employed, recently divorced, bankrupted in the last seven years, or have other credit challenges.

Third party financing fees can include, but are not limited to: the cost of points to lower the interest rate, origination fees, underwriting fees, appraisal fees, credit reports, title insurance, and more. All of these fees can result in thousands of dollars being added to the price of the home.

One of the biggest holdups in a property closing is financing. Buyers have to find a financier, provide mounds of documentation to prove their creditworthiness; and thereafter, the underwriting department calculates the risk associated with the buyer and decides whether the buyer will receive the financing. Financing can even fall through at the last minute; potentially ruining the home purchase for the buyer and the seller.

But this rigamaroo is a less of a factor when the seller provides the financing. When the seller is the financier, a buyer can close and move into a property within days, since there is no third party lender holding up the transaction.

Reduce Risk

Underwriting or lending to a buyers is definitely risky; there is always the chance that a buyer will default on or stop paying the mortgage loan. But there are steps that financing sellers can pursue to help diminish the liability from underwriting a mortgage loan.

As the financier, you decide how stringent to be regarding the buyer's credit. Traditional lending institutions attempt to limit risk by critically analyzing the creditworthiness of applicants and you can do the same.

Financing sellers can request that the buyer completes a detailed loan application and then thoroughly verify all of the buyer's information. Verifying and reviewing the buyer's credit, employment, assets, finances, references, and savings can definitely help better assess the buyer's creditworthiness. If the buyer does not seem creditworthy, do not offer seller financing.

If the buyer seems creditworthy, secure the loan through the property; this will allow a financing seller to foreclose on the property in the event the buyer defaults on the mortgage loan. Appraise the home to confirm its value is equal to or higher than the purchase price. The foreclosure process may require a lawyer and become expensive.

When extending seller financing, require a down payment from the buyer; this will provide an initial source of money and increase the buyer's stake in the property, hopefully making default less likely.

Interest rates can vary widely geographically; therefore, review local versus national rates. Offering a standard or low interest rate may help to attract buyers. Select an interest rate by comparing current rates of multiple lenders or reviewing the rates from websites like www.BankRate.com and www.HSH.com .

Financing sellers do not have to complete all of the work alone, there are loan servicing companies that can help. The loan servicing company can manage the mortgage by completing the required paperwork, mailing the statements to the buyers, and collecting the payments.

Title Company

In the purchase contract, buyers may request for the seller to pay for their title insurance. In most cities, there are a plethora of title companies to choose from, all of which provide the same services, more or less. You can call or visit the websites of a few title companies to get a better idea of what special services they provide and their fees.

In general, the title company conducts a thorough search to ensure the title is free, clear, and unencumbered. Title companies also may assist with the recording of new ownership information with the appropriate city, county, and state agencies. In the event there is a claim on the property, jeopardizing the lender's vested interest in the property, there is title insurance.

Title insurance protects the lender against title claims against the property, but this does not protect the buyer. To protect the buyer, there is owner's title insurance or an owner's policy. An owner's policy generally covers the amount of the real estate purchase for the duration of ownership of the property. The owner's policy protects the owner's interest should there be an issue with the title.

The owner's policy may cover:

- Forgery
- Undisclosed heirs
- Errors or omissions in deeds
- Mistakes in examining records

Home Warranty

A home warranty is a great feature to offer home buyers. Properly maintaining and repairing all of the appliances within a home can be costly, especially for a buyer who has just exhausted his or her savings on the purchase of a home.

A home warranty is a service contract that covers the repair and or replacement costs of home appliances and equipment such as plumbing and electrical components that fail due to normal use.

Generally there is an annual premium of $300 – 500 for a residential service contract. When service is needed, a payment or deductible is required. Most deductibles range from $35 - $100. Coverage varies significantly across home warranty companies. A home warranty policy should be reviewed carefully to determine the exact terms and what is specifically covered by the policy.

In addition, providing a home warranty may reduce the seller's liability and offer the buyer a sense of security knowing that should repairs be needed, a portion of the costs may be covered by the home warranty.

Closing Costs

Closing costs are a buyer's expense, but the buyer is already making a big purchase, which may require a significant outlay of funds. Helping the buyer with the closing costs may be what is necessary to close the deal. Paying for buyer's closing costs is more often seen in a buyer's market; nonetheless, assisting with the buyer's closing costs may be a great incentive for the buyer.

Closing costs can affect the amount of money that a buyer has for the purchase price of a property. Typically, a buyer will pay between approximately 2 – 5% of the property's purchase price in closing costs. If a home cost $150,000, closing costs may range between $3,000 and $7,500.

The price of the home may be increased to accommodate closing costs. Some sellers may request a full purchase offer to pay part or all of the closing costs. There are different stipulations associated with closing costs depending on the location, loan, and lender; on some occasions sellers can only partially pay for closing costs, while other times they can pay for all of them.

Typical closing costs may include the following fees:

- Survey fee
- Recording fee
- Title search fees
- Underwriting fee
- A credit report fee
- Title insurance fee
- Pest inspection fee
- Escrow deposit fee
- Discount points fee
- A loan origination fee
- Attorney's services fee
- Property inspection fee

Incentives can be highly motivating for some real estate agents and buyers. Review the incentives that you are interested in offering to help your property sell as fast possible for the greatest amount.

Action Steps

_____

_____

_____

_____

_____

_____

_____

_____

_____

_____

_____

_____

_____

_____

_____

_____

_____

_____

_____

_____

_____

_____

Chapter Seven
Marketing

This is the time to toot your horn; identify everything special about your property. In a buyer's market, your home may be competing with hundreds of properties. It is your job to tell the world what makes your property better than the other properties. Be specific; no detail is too small.

One of the most important attributes to home buyers is a home that is move-in ready or turn-key condition (NAR, 2013). After all, the buyer generally wants to move in. Not everyone has the time, energy, or desire to fix up a home before the move-in date.

When asked about the most important features of a home, buyers identified the following:

- Quality of:
  - Neighborhood
  - School district
- Proximity to:
  - Job
  - Airport
  - Schools
  - Shopping
  - Friends and family
  - Public transportation

- o Parks/Recreational facilities
- o Entertainment/Leisure activities
- ➤ Size of lot
- ➤ Planned community
- ➤ Affordability of home (NAR, 2013).

Coming Soon

Not quite ready to place your home on the market, but still want the world to know that it will be on the market soon? Place a "Coming Soon" sign in your front yard; the sign will alert buyers that your property will be on the market soon. The "Coming Soon" sign may help build buyers' anticipation to see your home. While the sign is out, continue to prepare your home for the market.

Energy Efficient

A market analysis of home sales revealed that energy efficient homes are more attractive to buyers than non-energy efficient homes. Homes classified as energy efficient sell faster and increase in value quicker. Some of the most notable energy upgrades include solar water heaters, geothermal heat pumps, spray foam insulation, and energy efficient windows and doors (NAR, 2013).

Whose Market?

The feigned control of the market is determined by who has an advantage in the real estate transaction; the buyer or the seller. A buyer's market exists when the supply of homes exceeds the buyers' demand for homes, which may give buyers the advantage in the purchase transaction.

A seller's market exists when there is a shortage in the supply of homes, which may increase the price of homes and create advantages for the sellers in the purchase transaction.

Listing Price

Sellers want to net the most money as possible from the sale of their property, while buyers want to pay the least amount of money for a property; herein lies the challenge.

Every home sale transaction is different, there is no way to predict with 100% certainty how long it will take to receive an offer and how much a buyer will offer, but there are ways to help improve the odds that an offer will arrive. There are many different approaches that sellers and real estate agents may use to price a home including the high, low, and right way.

Sellers have a lot of ideas about the listing price of their home. Popular options that sellers use to derive a listing price include, but are not limited to: tax appraised value, the amount needed to satisfy all liens plus a percentage, the original price plus a percentage–let's say 20% for market growth or appreciation, and rough estimates based off of observations of neighbors' properties.

Some people may think that a house can never be priced too low because the market will take care of it. Sellers and real estate agents may hope that a low-priced home will garner a lot of attention from buyers, ignite a bidding war, and drive up the price of the property–great fantasy. While this is an interesting strategy, it does not always pan out. Homes offered at a low-price may receive low purchase offers. To achieve an optimal price, review all of the information available to make the most informed decision.

Many sellers like the approach of pricing the property high, hoping for an offer, and adjusting the price in event an offer does not come in, which can be the kiss of death.

When prices start high and are lowered later, it is less likely that a seller will receive a good offer. When the sales price is lowered, buyers may wonder what's wrong with the property. If the property has been on the market for an extended period of time, buyers also may wonder what is wrong with the property.

It is important to know the current market conditions. A real estate agent should conduct a thorough market analysis to develop a good listing price. Real estate agents should review market data, which includes, but is not limited to: properties recently sold, properties currently on the market, and average days on market. Knowing the market conditions can help sellers and real estate agents determine a good price point of how much a buyer may be willing to pay.

Inaccurately pricing a home may cause a property to sit on the market for an extended period of time. It is important to carefully determine the best possible price to facilitate the property's sale. Carefully consider how long you want your house to sit on the market. A competitively-priced home generally will sale faster than high-priced home.

It is important to be realistic about the market value of a property. Creating unrealistic expectations regarding a property's value may further diminish the amount that a property may bring in. Idealistically, the home should be perfectly priced the moment it hits the market; not too high, not too low, just right.

Appraisal

The lender will most likely order an appraisal to determine the value of the property. Let's say the home is overpriced by 20%. Even if a buyer is willing to pay 20% more, the buyer may experience challenges when trying to get financing for the property. If a house does not appraise for at least the price identified in the purchase contract, the lender may not provide the buyer with financing for the property.

Foreclosures and distressed sales within your neighborhood may diminish the value of your house. Frequently real estate agents and appraisers quickly run numbers regarding the current market conditions of the neighborhood. A quick review of the market data may not adequately acknowledge extenuating circumstances of properties on the market and recently sold properties. In order to receive the best possible price, it is important that real estate agents and appraisers investigate any abnormal prices conditions. In some cases, a second appraisal may be necessary.

Unfortunately homes don't always appreciate, depreciation may occur. For example if John purchased and financed a home for a $100k, but five years later the home is valued at $85,000. Early in most mortgages, primarily interest is paid; therefore, John still owes $97,000. Over the last year, the highest price paid for a house in his neighborhood was $87,500 and the highest offer that John has received is $85,000. If John accepts the offer of 85,000, at closing John must satisfy the first lien of $97,000 by contributing $12,000; not to mention any additional fees.

Short Sales

An underwater situation results when the mortgage loan is higher than the price that a seller can get from placing a home on the market for sale. To prevent underwater situations, it is important that buyers do not overpay for a home and lenders do not over lend for a home.

When the sale of a home will not cover the amount owed by the seller, the seller must find additional funds to cover the difference to successfully repay the loan.

Defaulting on a loan is not a good idea. Defaulting on a loan can have negative effects on one's credit and even prohibit one from receiving credit or financing in the near future. In addition, some employers conduct credit checks before offering employment, so defaulting on a loan may even prevent one from obtaining or keeping a job.

Before defaulting on a loan, it is important to contact the lender to determine what alternatives may be offered. One alternative is a short sale. A short sale is generally a last resort. In most cases, the seller wants to sell the home, but the market value of the home will not sufficiently cover the lien or liens on the property.

The seller should contact the lender to inquire if the short sale process is available. If the lender will accept a short sale, it is important to inquire about the process and requirements. The short sale process can be lengthy. The purchase offer must be approved by the lender. In addition, there may be additional tax ramifications associated with any loan forgiveness by the lender.

Sellers Disclosure

The sellers' disclosure lists all known information about the house, especially any defects. Being upfront about any defects can help buyers decide if they want to pursue the purchase of your property and help avoid delays.

After a purchase contract is written, most buyers will order a property inspection. The property inspection may reveal a lot of information about the property, including any defects.

Exposing all of a property's known defects before the buyers order an inspection may diffuse their anxiety about the property and may reduce any surprises resulting from the inspection. Learning about flaws after an inspection may cause buyers to abandon a purchase contract.

Photos

Before the photographer takes one photo, make sure that your home is picture perfect. The home should be staged and well-lit to help the home photograph well.

A picture definitely is worth a thousand words, make sure your marketing materials are stocked with plenty of great photos of the property. Many buyers will look at property photos online or presented by their real estate agent before actually visiting a property.

Generally, the best exterior photo is selected to showcase the home in marketing material. If a fantastic exterior photo is not available, consider using the best interior photo of the property.

Amenities

If your house has really great features like a 18th century chandelier or a fresco painting in the children's room–let buyers know. While the listing paperwork may seem to go on forever, take the time to be as specific as possible. Your real estate agent should lists these special items to encourage interest from buyers.

Open House

Holding an open house is a good opportunity to showcase one's home to the public, but don't expect any miracles; open houses generally are only successful at creating a home sale 2-5% of the time (NAR, 2013).

Brochures

The buyers just left your house and searched every nook and cranny. Why on earth would the buyers need a brochure? Keep in mind that most home buyers are generally looking at multiple properties. It is important to do everything that you can to help the buyers remember your property, and a brochure can help accomplish this goal.

In addition to great photos of your property, the brochure can include information about appliances, recent updates, antiques, and seller financing, if it is available.

Not Included

If it is attached to the house, it is considered part of the house and it will be part of the sale of the property. If there is something special that you want from the house, remove it before the house goes on the market; this will help to resolve quibbles about who gets what.

For example, your grandmother's chandelier—you have every intention of taking it when you move, but it is hanging in the dining room until then. Incidentally, the buyer has fallen in love with the chandelier and insists that it be left in the house; after all, it is attached to the house. This is a potentially messy situation that can be avoided.

If you are interested in removing a special fixture or another item from the house, remove it before the property is placed on the market. In addition, consider selecting a suitable replacement.

Sellers have the option to sale items within the house for additional money. Items offered for sale generally include, but are not limited to: refrigerators, clothes washers, and clothes dryers.

If any attached item will be removed from the property, but is still attached, it should be clearly defined in the property's marketing materials and listing information.

Schools

Schools can be very important incentives to buyers with children. If your home is close to great schools, don't forget to mention it to your real estate agent. In addition, school boundaries can change. Double check with the school district to ensure that there have not been any changes made to the school boundaries.

Landmarks

Being in close proximity to high-interest areas can be very attractive to buyers. If your home is near a special attraction, make sure this information is included in all marketing information.

Properly marketing a property is crucial. Sellers may be looking for exactly what you are offering, but if it is not specifically identified and announced; how will they know? They won't. Take the time to let your real estate agent and the rest of the world know about all of the great features of your home to create interest and maximize marketing efforts.

Action Steps

_____

_____

_____

_____

_____

_____

_____

_____

_____

_____

_____

_____

_____

_____

_____

_____

_____

_____

_____

_____

_____

_____

Chapter Eight
The Showing

It is here! The moment that you have been preparing for–the showing! This is when your home is shown to buyers in hopes of being purchased. Even after you have depersonalized, decluttered, cleaned, fixed, and inspected there are a few more steps to help ensure that your home shows well.

Get out!

Staying inside of the home while it is shown may prevent buyers from truly being comfortable and looking around, so it is important that you vacate the property.

Security

Yes, the buyers are going to snoop and go through all of your personal stuff, so get ready. Anything that is too private or valuable should be removed from the property to a more secure location, especially small expensive pieces. As you are packing up everything, secure your valuables and get them ready for their new home.

In addition to jewelry, another popular theft item is medication. Yes–people will enter your home under the premise of wanting to buy it and may attempt to steal your medication; avoid this by securing your medication in a safe location.

When selling one's home, security can be challenging because real estate agents and buyers will enter and view the home. This may cause the need to disable the home's alarm system. Some alarm systems may have multiple access codes, allowing the homeowner to keep a private access code, while assigning another access to code to the listing agent to share with buyer's agents.

Hidden cameras offer another level of security to sellers. A motion activated hidden camera can provide additional information about what is going on inside of your home when you are not there.

Buyers will go in and out of every door, upon returning to the property it is important to check that all doors are safely secured. Keeping your home safe and secure is paramount. Be sure to take every precaution to safeguard your belongings while your home is on the market.

Smell

Nothing should distract the buyer's focus from your house, especially not a smell. Many people are highly sensitive to smells. Foods, especially meats and special herbs and spices, can be especially fragrant and noisome to some individuals. In addition, food odors can linger and they may be offensive to the senses. Don't let residual smells of food drive away your buyers.

If you cook foods that have strong smells, take steps to alleviate the smells created by the foods. Strong smells can be lessened by cooking with a fan on, opening a window or a door to bring in fresh air, and using air neutralizers to eliminate odors.

Smells of old smoke from cigarettes, cigars, and other smokeables can be especially offensive and intolerable to some buyers. If you enjoy smoking, consider doing it outside while your home is on the market.

In attempt to cover smells and create an enticing fragrance, be careful not to overdo it. Strong fragrances, even pleasant ones, can be especially bothersome to some people. Carefully select the scents and or deodorizers used in the property. Also keep in mind that some people may be allergic to certain scents and fragrances. To stay on the safe side, lightly use scents and fragrances.

Trash

Essentially you are trying to create the feeling of a perfect model home; a home that is eagerly awaiting the arrival of a new homeowner. Nothing says old and lived in more than a can of stinky trash. Before you go to bed every night or before you leave every morning; make sure that you empty all trash into a large closed receptacle outdoors.

Utilities

It may be tempting to save a couple of dollars by turning off the air conditioning or even the utilities while you are not in the property, but it is important that the property be shown in all of its glory, which is not possible when some of the home's features or utilities are turned off.

Buyers should be comfortable. If it is cold outside make the property warm and inviting. If it is hot outside, make the property cool and refreshing. Uncomfortable temperatures within the property may cause buyers to leave early and prevent them from truly experiencing the wonderfulness of the home, so make sure the temperature is inviting.

In addition, the property inspector will most likely need all of the utilities turned on; therefore, make sure the property is fully functional during any property inspection.

Light & Bright

Don't expect each real estate agent to come in and light up your home, try to leave it perfectly lit. When showing your home, consider turning on every light in the house, including the appliance and closet lights. Opening all of the window treatments is a great way to naturally brighten the home. If a room still doesn't look bright enough, consider getting additional lamps.

In addition to having a well-lit interior, don't forget about the exterior. Some buyers visit and view properties after work, in the evening. Depending on the time of year, it can get dark pretty early. Lighting up the exterior can be as easy as placing solar lights along the side walk and keeping the porch light on.

Technology Assisted

While keeping the lights on may help a property show well to buyers, it is not energy efficient nor cost effective, but technology can help. Motion sensing lights or timers can be utilized inside and outside of the property to help maximize electrical efficiency while showcasing your home.

Animals

Pet owners really love their pets, and that's sweet. But the rest of the world may not be in love with Fluffy or Fido. Some people are even desperately allergic to pet hair and even being in the same room that a dog had been in hours or days before may cause an colossal allergic reaction.

Others who are not allergic to cats and dogs may be afraid of them. Who could be afraid of your harmless cuddly Cujo? Plenty of people.

Leaving your animals outside is not a solution; it may prevent buyers from exploring the exterior of the property. Consider making alternative arrangements for your precious pets. Perhaps friends, family, or a pet hotel will accommodate your little friend until the sale of your property is finalized.

Cleaning Service

A cleaning service can be instrumental in helping to get the property prepared for the market and remain ready to be on the market. It is often necessary for the seller to declutter and remove as much furniture and personal affects as possible before the home is even ready for a cleaning service. A cleaning service can definitely help busy sellers keep their home ready for visiting buyers at a moment's notice.

Keep It Open

Cleaning and getting ready to move can definitely be challenging. Who needs another expense of getting a storage unit, why not just put all of the junk in a spare room or the garage? After all, you've seen one spare room or one garage, you've seen them all right?

Wrong. Buyers want to see all of the rooms. It doesn't matter if it is just a spare room or the garage. When rooms are locked, buyers may start to imagine that something is wrong or they may want to see it even more just because the door is locked. Lessen buyers' doubts and curiosity; provide them with the most complete picture of your home as possible–keep everything open.

Music

A little light music can be a welcomed addition while buyers are viewing your property. Consider playing music in the background, nothing too loud or edgy; just a little music to fill the house and to make the showing more enjoyable.

Information Station

An information station can be instrumental in selling a home. An information station should be centrally located and easily identifiable to the buyers. Information stations are frequently located on a counter or table in the kitchen or a small table by the front entrance. The information station can request real estate agents' cards, and feedback from the buyers and real estate agents about their opinion of the property. The information station can also provide a property brochure.

Leaving a bowl of treats filled with small pieces of candy or chocolate can be a nice addition to the information station and may help encourage buyers to leave feedback. Don't forget to leave a small trash receptacle nearby.

Feedback is an essential part of the selling process; it is important to constantly evaluate your efforts to sale the property. Sometimes sellers can be too close to their property, which may prevent them from seeing obvious needs for improvements.

There are many actions that a seller can take to help his or her property show well. Take advantage of all of the strategies available to improve the odds of getting a good offer quickly. The information and feedback left by the real estate agents and buyers should be reviewed as quickly as possible to help facilitate the sale of the property.

Action Steps

_____

_____

_____

_____

_____

_____

_____

_____

_____

_____

_____

_____

_____

_____

_____

_____

_____

_____

_____

_____

Chapter Nine
Offer & Closing

How Long?

Your home has had multiple showings, but no contracts. What gives? Keep in mind that not everyone who visits your property will be in the position to buy it; unfortunately not all home lookers are homebuyers. Nonetheless, it is important to have patience until an offer comes in.

While it is important not to be too anxious, it is also important to watch how much time is passing by. If after several weeks, there has not been any interest expressed in the property, it may be time to revisit the property to see what can be improved or adjusted to increase interest and facilitate the sale of the property.

As the price of the home increases, the number of buyers who can afford the home decreases, which in some cases may cause the home to stay on the market for an extended period of time.

For instance, almost 100% of homebuyers may be able to purchase a home priced at $20,000. This does not mean that it will sell fast, it just mean that price is less of a factor. Versus a million dollar property; there are definitely fewer buyers who can buy or even finance a million dollar mortgage loan.

Seasons also have the ability to affect home sales. Many people prefer to move during the summer. During the summer moving conditions may be better; children are out of school, the weather may be warm and sunny, and other people are moving as well.

Keep in mind that if you have selected to move during an off peak moving season, your home may spend additional time on the market.

Anyone can want to buy a home, but may not be able to afford it. Before wasting precious days removing your home from market, require a pre-approval letter from the buyer's lender with the purchase contract. The pre-approval letter can help you determine if a buyer actually has the funds to purchase your home.

Buyers may submit a pre-qualification letter, but this is not good enough. Pre-qualification is one of the first steps in the mortgage process. The buyer, also known as the borrower, supplies the lender with information regarding his or her debt, income, and assets, and the lender provides an estimate of how much the buyer may qualify for. During the pre-qualification process, a lender does not verify any of the borrowers' information; therefore, the pre-qualification letter is only as valid as the information provided by the borrower. If one piece of information is wrong or withheld, the conditions of the pre-qualification letter can dramatically change.

A pre-approval is generally a written conditional commitment from the lender. Generally borrowers will complete an official mortgage application and supply the lender with an abundance of information. The lender will also conduct an extensive financial and credit check. Based on all of the information the lender receives, the lender will draft a pre-approval letter that details how much a borrower is approved for.

Buyers can get a loan commitment after the lender approves the buyer and the property. The lender will generally require that the home appraises at or above the purchase price.

A buyer's loan commitment does have an expiration date, so make sure the title company schedules the closing before the expiration date.

Once a legitimate offer arrives with the lender's pre-approval letter, the real estate agent will forward you the offer. Now it is time to review the offer with a fine tooth comb. Each line item in the contract has the ability to change the amount that you will net.

If after reviewing every aspect of the contract you are satisfied with the offer, sign it, and return it to your real estate agent. Depending on the particulars identified in the contract, the listing agent will change the status of your home from **Available** to **Pending Show**, **Option Pending**, or **Pending**.

Pending Show signifies that there is a pending purchase contract on the property, and the buyer and seller are waiting for the property to close, but the property is still available for showings. Sometimes offers do not go through for a variety of reasons. Pending Show still allows buyers the opportunity to view the property with the understanding that the property has a contract.

The Pending Show status also gives buyers the opportunity to submit backup contracts. Whereas, the property has an initial contract, and a second buyer may submit a contract in the event that the first contract does not go through; more often seen in a seller's market or a highly sought after property or neighborhood.

Some buyer's agents will not even consider showing a property that has a Pending Show status because there is a strong chance that the transaction will be finalized. Most buyer's agents may believe that it would be more beneficial to focus on homes that are available; not under contract.

Option Pending is a status that signifies that a home is currently in the option period. This is generally a ten-day period that allows the buyer to carefully consider the offer to purchase the property and order a property inspection. The property inspector comes out to the property, conducts a thorough inspection, and provides a detailed report of the property's condition to the buyer. Depending on the findings and details of the inspection report, the buyer may decide to proceed or exercise the option to void the purchase contract.

If all of the repairs are made before the home is placed on the market, the inspector's report will most likely have fewer surprises and negative incidences, leaving the buyer with less to contemplate.

The **Pending** status signifies that the property is under a contract, is not in the option period, the property is not available for showings, and that finalization of the sale of the property is imminent.

Offers

Fingers crossed, an offer will arrive before you know it. Once the offer arrives there are many variables to consider. What if the offer is too low or the buyer is asking for too much? Should you accept, negotiate, or reject the offer?

One of the seller's primary concerns is the profit from the property sale. Many sellers frequently say, "I want to get my money back from the property."

Unfortunately all offers are not full price; buyers can offer any amount to purchase a property. For instance, you may receive an offer $5,000 short of your asking price. Your first knee jerk reaction may be to reject the offer in hopes of a full price offer.

If you are insistent upon only accepting a specified amount for a purchase offer, determine if it is realistic to maintain this goal. Does the market analysis support the price? Also, look at other homes for sale in the neighborhood. How does your property compare?

If the property has been listed for a short period of time, perhaps a couple of weeks, rejecting an offer may not be the worst idea. Perhaps there may be a better offer soon. But if the property has been listed for six months, it might be a good idea to seriously consider the offer.

Sellers have turned down offers a couple thousand short of their ideal price to go months without receiving another offer. If you are positively OK with keeping your property indefinitely, reject an unfavorable offer. If you are not OK with keeping your property indefinitely, consider giving an offer a second look or presenting a counter offer.

Accepting a lower purchase price can be less than ideal, but every offer deserves consideration. Determine if you can accept the offer. Evaluate how long it took to receive this offer. How much does it cost to keep the property? Consider mortgage payments, taxes, maintenance, homeowner association fees, and more.

The future is unknown and it goes back to the adage: a bird in the hand is worth more than two in the bush. Who knows when the next offer will arrive.

Negotiating

If you receive an offer that you don't like, consider negotiating with the buyer. Carefully evaluate each part of the offer to determine the salient points of the deal. Decide what you want to negotiate.

Be careful when you haggle over nickels and dimes, or even a few thousand dollars; you may potentially lose the purchase offer. If you feel as though you are giving away the farm and just can't live with the deal, determine what can make the deal more palatable to you. Perhaps the buyer may be willing to make some concessions.

Rejection

When the offer is just not acceptable or you are not interested in proposing a counteroffer; reject the offer. But don't alienate a buyer who is interested in purchasing your property. Invite the buyer to submit another purchase offer. The seller or the listing agent can share with the buyer the terms that the seller will find more favorable.

Back on the Market

Unfortunately, not all purchase contracts successfully close. There are a variety of reasons why a property sale transaction may not be finalized including, but not limited to: buyer's remorse, negative findings identified in the property inspection report, issues with the financing, and buyers unable to sell their current property before closing on the next property.

Contract

After the contract is executed, whereas the buyer and the seller have both agreed to the terms of the purchase contract, it can definitely feel like a mad dash to get everything completed before closing. To help avoid the rush, you can start collecting and compiling all of the required documents as soon as possible.

To identify all of the required documents, contact a title company. Some sellers select a title company before the home receives an offer; however, *a seller cannot require a buyer to use a specific title company per Section 9 of the Real Estate Settle Procedure Act.*

Receipts and Warranties

Create a folder to deposit all the receipts and warranties that you have for the appliances and repairs in the property. This can be valuable to the buyers and may help them fix any conditions that arise within the property.

Home Warranty

As mentioned in chapter six, the home warranty is a nice feature to provide to a buyer. A home warranty can be funded at closing to help ensure the buyer has a service contract on some of the appliances and equipment in the home. Different service companies offer varying premiums, deductibles, and coverage, so it is important to review more than one service company to find the best offerings.

HOA Packet

If your home belongs to a homeowners association (HOA), this information should be provided to the buyer. This information may have an expiration date; so check with the title company and HOA to ensure that all requirements have been met.

Survey

A property survey is generally required at most closings to provide clarity about the property location. A property survey contains specific information about the borders of the property. In addition to the information about the boundaries, property surveys may provide information about easements. Easements specify one's ability to use land that is not owned.

For instance, there are two properties; one in the front and one in the back. A driveway crosses over the property in the front to reach the house in the back. The easement gives the property owner in the back the right to use the driveway, even without ownership.

As long as there has not been any changes in the boundaries of the property, providing an existing survey may be beneficial to the buyer by eliminating the need to purchase a new survey.

HUD-1

Before the closing date, request for the title company to send you a preliminary HUD-1. The HUD-1 is a settlement statement that itemizes the fees of the buyer and seller in a real estate transaction. The HUD-1 gives a description of all of the expenses, but this sheet is not infallible. Carefully review HUD-1 to ensure that all line items are correct. Reviewing the HUD-1 early will allow you to double check questionable line items with the title company.

Closing

After you sell your home, the title company will give you a packet of information. Of course you are going to place this packet of information in a safe place; you may need to refer to this information when completing your taxes or another activity.

If you haven't already decided, you need to consider where you are going to move. Are you going to rent, lease, or buy? Give yourself the opportunity to carefully consider your living arrangement. Renting or leasing may give you the time to select the perfect property. While buying can give you the opportunity to make an investment and a more permanent living arrangement.

Either way, it is time to contact those who you do business with to inform them of your new address; you don't want all of your important mail and information to continually be sent to your old address.

Action Steps

_____

_____

_____

_____

_____

_____

_____

_____

_____

_____

_____

_____

_____

_____

_____

_____

_____

_____

_____

Hello Seller,

I hope that you have found the information in this book helpful.
If you have any questions please send me an e-mail.

Happy selling,

Jessica deValentino

DeValentino Properties LLC
www.devalentino.com
j@devalentino.com
Houston, Texas

References

2013 Profile of Home Buyers and Sellers. (2013). *National Association of Realtors*.

Field Guide to Quick Real Estate Statistics. (2014, July 1). *National Association of Realtors*.

The benefits of plants (2014). Ambius. Retrieved from June 8, 2014 from http://www.ambius.com/learn/benefits-of-our-services/

Appendix A
Cleaning Supply List

When shopping for cleaning supplies, it can be easy to forget an item or two at the store. Below you find a list of almost everything that you may need to help your home sparkle. The list can also be downloaded from www.devalentino.com .

DeValentino Properties LLC ♦ 281.682.8688 ♦ j@devalentino.com ♦ www.devalentino.com

Cleaning Supplies

Air filters	Microfiber cloth
Air freshener	Microfiber mop
All-purpose cleaner	Mop
Baking soda	Mop bucket
Bleach	Muriatic acid
Boxes, packing	Oven cleaner
Broom	Oven mitts
Bucket	Paper towels
Cleaning cloths	Plastic tote
Deodorizers	Scouring pads, stainless steel or mesh
Dish detergent	Silver or metal Polish
Dishwasher detergent	Sponges
Dryer sheets	Stone cleaner
Duster	Tissues
Dustpan	Toilet bowl cleaner
Extendible duster	Toilet brush
Gel scents	toilet paper
Glass cleaner	Trash can liners
Gloves, gardening	Trash cans (for area of the house)
Gloves, plastic	Upholstery spot remover
Grout brush	Vacuum
Kitchen towels	Vacuum bag
Laundry detergent	Vinegar
Laundry stain remover	Window cleaner
Leather cleaner	Wood polish
Mesh scrubber	

Appendix B:
Daily Cleaning Checklist

Download the sheet below from www.devalentino.com

DeValentino Properties LLC ♦ 281.682.8688 ♦ j@devalentino.com ♦ www.devalentino.com

House Cleaning Checklist   Date

Kitchen	M	T	W	T	F
Clean counters					
Clean int/ext appliances					
Clean int/ext fridge					
Clean int/ext microwave					
Clean range, vent, & filter					
Clean windows/treatments					
Organize table setting					
Polish stainless steel					
Sweep and cleanse floor					

Dining Room	M	T	W	T	F
Clean chairs					
Clean windows/treatments					
Organize table settings					
Sweep/vac./cleanse floor					

Bathroom	M	T	W	T	F
Clean/polish fixtures					
Clean/sanitize shower					
Clean/sanitize sinks					
Clean/sanitize toilet					
Clean/sanitize tub					
Dust light fixtures & bulbs					
Dust/cleanse baseboards					
Sweep/cleanse floor					

Bedrooms	M	T	W	T	F
Change sheets					
Dust furniture/shelves					
Dust lights fixture					
Empty wastebaskets					
Put away laundry					
Sweep/vacuum floor					
Wash windows/treatments					

Front Yard	M	T	W	T	F
Organize materials					
Rake/sweep outdoors					
Trim grass/shrubs/trees					

Living Room	M	T	W	T	F
Clean windows/treatments					
Dust furniture					
Polish furniture					
Sweep/vacuum/mop floor					
Vacuum furniture					

Study/Office	M	T	W	T	F
Clean windows/treatments					
Dust furniture					
File or toss papers					
Polish/clean surfaces					
Sweep/vacuum/mop floor					
Vacuum furniture					

Entry/Halls/Stairs	M	T	W	T	F
Clean windows/treatments					
Dust/ceiling & baseboards					
Sweep/vacuum/mop floors					

Laundry/Utility Room	M	T	W	T	F
Clean counters & hampers					
Clean ext. washer/dryer					
Clean fixtures					
Clean inside of washer					
Clean lint trap					
Empty garbage					
Sweep/vacuum/mop floor					

Garage	M	T	W	T	F
Empty garbage					
Organize shelves					
Sweep floor					

Backyard	M	T	W	T	F
Empty trash					
Trim grass/shrubs/trees					
Rake/sweep outdoors					
Organize outdoor furniture					

Appendix C
Net Sheet

Download the sheet below from www.devalentino.com

SELLER'S ESTIMATED NET PROCEEDS
DeValentino Properties LLC
www.devalentino.com ♦ 281.682.8688 ♦ j@devalentino.com

The figures below may help to develop estimates; actual costs and proceeds may vary.

Estimated Net Proceeds	$
Sales Price	
Less Estimated Costs	
Less Estimated Loan Payoff	
Estimated Net Proceeds	

Costs	$
Attorney's Fees	
Condo. Transfer Fee	
Doc. Prep Fees	
Escrow Fee	
Prorated Assessments	
Prorated Interest	
Prorated Maintenance Fees	
Prorated Rents	
Prorated Taxes	
Recording fees	
Repairs Required by Buyer	
Repairs required by Lender	
Residential Service Contract	
Seller Allowances	
Survey fee	
Tax Certificate Fee	
Title / Owner's Fee	
Wiring Fees	
Total	

Appendix D
Deep Cleaning Checklist

Of course you know how to clean your home. This is just a list to help you track your cleaning efforts and reduce the likelihood of overlooking any important areas of the home. Happy cleaning!

FOYER
1. Dust light fixtures.
2. Wash walls, trim, and light plates.
3. Wash doors and knobs.
4. Empty and organize coat closet.
5. Remove knick-knacks.
6. Clean or replace the welcome mat.
7. Sweep, cleanse, and or vacuum floors.
8. Paint, if necessary.

BEDROOMS
1. Open windows.
2. Dust furniture.
3. For each drawer:
    i. Remove items.
    ii. Wash drawer.
    iii. Replace items neatly.
4. Donate or throw away unneeded items.
5. Closets:
    i. Remove everything
    ii. Sweep, cleanse, and or vacuum floors.
    iii. Put everything back neatly.
    iv. Donate unneeded items.
    v. Try not to store things on closet floor or shelves.

6. Bed:
    i. Move bed.
    ii. Sort and organize items under the bed.
    iii. Sweep or vacuum under bed.
    iv. Try not to store items under bed.
7. Mattress: freshen by sprinkling with baking soda, wait briefly, and vacuum.
8. Launder bedding, curtains, pillows, and duvet.
9. Dust lights and lamp shades.
10. Wash windows, window sills, and screens.
11. Wash walls, trim, and light plates, as needed.
12. Wash mirrors or dust frame.
13. Wash doors and doorknobs.
14. Wash floor registers and vent covers.
15. Sweep, cleanse, or vacuum floors.
16. Clean blades of ceiling fans.

BATHROOMS
1. Open windows, if possible.
2. Cabinets and vanity.
    1. Empty.
    2. Wash inside and outside.
    3. Replace items neatly.
3. Discard expired medications and cosmetics.
4. Clean tub and drain.
5. Clean toilet; inside and out.
6. Remove the toilet seat and clean around seat bolts.
7. Cleanse sink, faucets, and drain.
8. Clean mirror and dust frame.
9. Wash windows, window sills, and screens.
10. Wash light plates, trim, and walls.
11. Wash doors and door knobs.
12. Sweep, cleanse, or vacuum floors.

13. Reseal grout lines if necessary.

Shower doors can be especially challenging to clean. Consider a combination 10 parts water to 1 part muriatic acid to get a dazzling sparkle from dismal and dirty shower doors. Scrub any residual grime off with steel wool. Be careful, muriatic acid is highly corrosive and does not work well with steel wool. Muriatic acid can be purchased at most hardware and home improvement stores.

Mix equal parts bleach and water, and spray the wall to remove mold from most surfaces in the bathroom.

KITCHEN
1. Open windows, if possible.
2. Remove and clean window coverings.
3. Cabinet or drawer:
    1. Remove items.
    2. Wipe out drawer.
    3. Return items neatly.
4. Wash cabinet inside and out.
5. Pantry:
    1. Discard expired food.
    2. Clean and organize.
6. Clean oven.
7. Clean stovetop; clean elements and drip bowls, if needed.
8. Fridge and freezer.
    1. Discard expired food.
    2. Defrost freezer, if necessary.
    3. Clean and organize.
9. Clean under fridge and stove.
10. Clean or vacuum refrigerator coils.

11. Clean microwave.

12. Clean crumbs out of toaster.

13. Clean and descale kettle.

14. Wipe down all counter appliances.

15. Wash counters and back splash.

16. Wash and shine sink, faucet, and drain.

17. Clean dishwasher, especially bottom.

18. Dust light fixtures.

19. Wash windows, window sills, and screens.

20. Wash trim, light plates, and walls, as needed.

21. Wash doors and door knobs.

22. Wash floor registers and vent covers

23. Sweep, cleanse, or vacuum floors.

DINING ROOM

1. Open windows.

2. Cleanse window treatments.

3. Wipe down table and chairs.

4. Wipe down or dust other furnishing.

5. Clean chair pads, if applicable.

6. Polish table, if necessary.

7. Dust place settings.

8. Launder linens.

9. Shine silverware.

10. Dust art.

11. Wash windows, window sills, and screens.

12. Wash walls, trim, and light plates.

13. Wash doors and door knobs.

14. Wash floor registers and other vent covers.

15. Sweep, cleanse, or vacuum floors.

LIVING ROOM / FAMILY ROOM / PLAYROOM

1. Open windows.

2. Vacuum and spot clean sofas, if necessary.

3. Launder throw pillows and blankets.
4. Dust shelves, furniture, and decor.
5. Clean lamps and lampshades.
6. Wash windows, window sills, and screens.
7. Dust and clean television screen.
8. Carefully dust electronics.
9. Tidy electronics wires.
10. Discard unused items.
11. Organize books and magazines; donate or recycle excess.
12. Toys
    1. Wash and sanitize plastic toys.
    2. Launder stuffed toys.
    3. Donate or store toys.
13. Wash walls, trim, and light plates, as needed.
14. Wash doors and knobs.
15. Wash floor registers and vent covers.
16. Sweep, cleanse, or vacuum floors.

LAUNDRY ROOM

1. Open windows, if possible.
2. Wash windows, window sills, and screens.
3. Wash outside and inside of cabinets.
4. Cleanse laundry sink, faucet, and drains.
5. Cleanse inside and outside of washer and dryer.
6. Wash walls, trim, and light plates, as needed.
7. Wash doors and door knobs.
8. Wash floor registers and vent covers.
9. Sweep, cleanse, or vacuum floors.

STAIR

1. Sweep and vacuum stairs.
2. Spot clean walls.
3. Wipe down handrail.

4. Dust art and light fixtures.

OUTSIDE
1. Sweep porches and walkways.
2. Wash thresholds.
3. Wash exterior doors. Paint, if needed.
4. Clean or replace welcome mat.
5. Power wash exterior, if needed.

REMEMBER TO:
- Clean blades of ceiling fans.
- Sort and organize documents and files.
- Sort and clean any extra zones such as linen closets, utility closets, and the office.

Appendix E:

Green Clean

Commercial cleaners do an excellent job of cleaning and disinfecting, but sometimes you may want a greener and economical alternative. White distilled vinegar is an effective cleaner that may eliminate most mold, bacteria, and germs, due to its high acidity. In addition, white distilled vinegar helps one avoid using harsh chemicals. Some uses of white distilled vinegar include, but are not limited to:

Shine chrome sink fixtures that have a lime buildup by using a paste made of 2 tablespoons baking soda and 1 teaspoon white distilled vinegar.

Make a scouring cleanser by combining 1/4 cup baking soda, 1 tablespoon liquid soap, and enough white distilled vinegar to give it a thick, but creamy texture.

Clean and deodorize a drain or garbage disposal by pouring in 1 cup baking soda and one cup hot white distilled vinegar. Let the mixture sit for approximately 5 minutes and then run hot water down the drain.

Remove soap, mineral, grease, and odors from the dishwasher by pouring a cup of white distilled vinegar inside the empty machine and running it through a whole cycle every couple of weeks.

To prevent hard water buildup on glassware, spray clean glasses with full-strength white distilled vinegar, rinse with hot water, and air or towel dry.

Get rid of lime deposits in tea kettles and cups by soaking in white distilled vinegar and scrubbing with baking soda. To enhance effectiveness, heat vinegar and soak for an extended period of time.

Remove mineral deposits from coffee makers with white distilled vinegar. Fill the water reservoir with 1 cup or more of white distilled vinegar and run it through a whole cycle. Run it once or twice more with plain water to rinse clean. (Review the owners' manual first)

Remove smells and light stains on plastic food containers by soaking them in white distilled vinegar.

Discourage ants by spraying undiluted white distilled vinegar outside doorways and windowsills, around appliances, and wherever you find the pests entering.

Get rid of fruit flies by setting out a small dish of undiluted white distilled vinegar or apple cider vinegar. Some fruit flies may collect on the exterior of the glass. Place a large container over the whole glass until all of the flies have taken their final flight.

Get rid of calcium deposits on faucets and showerheads by soaking a cloth or paper towel in white distilled vinegar and wrapping the area tightly. Keep the area wrapped for a couple of hours or overnight. Shine by scrubbing faucets with a solution of 1 part baking soda to 4 parts white distilled vinegar. For intense mineral deposits, tie a plastic or sandwich bag containing white distilled vinegar around it. Leave the area soaking for two or three hours. Scrub with baking soda to remove any remaining residue.

Shine no-wax vinyl or linoleum floor by cleansing with a solution of one cup white distilled vinegar for every gallon of water.

Clean carpet stains with a paste of 2 tablespoons white distilled vinegar and 1/4 cup or baking soda. Scrub the carpet stain and let dry. Vacuum up the residue the next day. (Spot test on a small portion first)

Remove white water rings from wood with a solution of equal parts white distilled vinegar and vegetable oil. Rub with the grain. **DO NOT use with waxed wood. It can ruin the finish and leave a cloudy mark.**

Avoid using white distilled vinegar on marble. The acid in the vinegar can dull and damage the surface.

Deodorize mattresses by lightly spraying white distilled vinegar and water solution on the mattress and then sprinkle with baking soda. Let the mixture dry. Remove the mixture by sweeping it off the bed or vacuuming the residue.

Other Titles from the Publisher

How to Lose Weight in The Real World: Why Other Diets Suck and You're Not Losing Weight (2010)
This is not your traditional diet book; HLWRW aims to help people gain a better understanding of their dietary decisions and how dietary decisions fit in with everyday life. The book addresses: (1) the basis of many popular fad diets and why they will not work for most people, (2) how seemingly harmless foods may sabotage good health (3) the extent of help that is available for those who need help (4) the importance of adding certain foods to your diet, and (5) ways to promote health through lifestyle choices.

Brainiac (2014)
Brainiac is a comical children's book about Emmie and her friends' frustration at earning low grades in school. But in swoops Brainiac to the rescue, revealing his top-secret strategies to learning more and earning better grades in school.

www.ingramcontent.com/pod-product-compliance
Lightning Source LLC
Chambersburg PA
CBHW071622040426
42452CB00009B/1448